SCHIRMER'S LIBRARY OF MUSICAL CLASSICS

Vol. 1663

NICCOLO PAGANINI

Op. 1

Twenty-Four Caprices

For the Violin

Study-Version and Preface

by

HAROLD BERKLEY

G. SCHIRMER, Inc.

DISTRIBUTED BY
HAL•LEONARD®
CORPORATION
7777 W. BLUEMOUND RD. P.O. BOX 13819 MILWAUKEE, WI 53213

PREFACE

In the last hundred years many excellent studies have been written for the development of the higher technique of violin playing—particularly those of Dont, Vieuxtemps, De Bériot, Wieniawski, and Sauret. Topping them all, however, the Twenty-four Caprices of Paganini still remain the one indispensable factor in the acquirement of genuine virtuosity.

Actually, the player should have a considerable degree of virtuosity before he attempts them. Many ambitious students, realizing the value of the Caprices and influenced by the glamor that has attached itself to the name of Paganini, undertake to study them without sufficient preparation—often going directly to them after studying the Rode Caprices. This is not the method by which the best results may be obtained. Before taking up the Paganini Caprices the student should have carefully and thoroughly studied the 24 Caprices of Dont, Op. 35, the first book of the De Bériot 60 Studies, and at least some of the "Grandes Études" of Sauret. In fact, this may be considered the minimum preparation necessary for intelligent study of the Paganini Caprices.

The student must realize clearly that these Twenty-four Caprices are a great deal more than exercises in advanced left-hand technique. Most of them are compositions of real musical value, and to give expression to their inherent qualities requires not only a finished left-hand technique but also an agile and sensitively controlled bow-arm—plus the imaginative ability to imbue technical passage-work with life and color.

The difficulties encountered by the left hand often lead the player to overlook the exacting demands made on his right arm, with the result that one frequently hears performances of the Caprices in which the general effect is muddy despite an immaculate finger technique. Many of them are as valuable for developing artistic control of the bow as they are for increasing the technical ability of the fingers. The student who has trained his bowing along modern lines*, and who has absorbed all that can be learned about bowing from the 60 Studies of De Bériot, will be ready for the problems that confront him in these Caprices—and will, moreover, be prepared to derive the utmost benefit from them.

It hardly needs to be said that the player must concentrate on acquiring complete control of technique, especially intonation, before he gives much attention to musical interpretation. On the other hand, he must realize that the ability to play the notes easily will not of itself result in a satisfactory performance.

The final worth of the Caprices is realized only when the difficulties of the left hand are completely mastered, for then the player may concern himself entirely with the fusion of pure technique with musical eloquence—which is the ultimate goal of the artist.

In the following pages many of the expression marks are those of the editor, as Paganini inserted comparatively few. They are given as a guide to the student in developing his own interpretations, and may be disregarded if he finds a plan of expression more suited to his own individuality.

The square notes (◻) given in some of the Caprices indicate Advance Fingering—i.e., the placing of a finger on the string in preparation for a note which immediately follows. When this device becomes an automatic part of the player's technique, it greatly increases both solidity and fluency of fingering.

The tempo indications, also, have been supplied by the editor, and can be considered as approximately indicating the tempo at which, in the hands of a skilled player, the musical content of each Caprice may best be given expression.

NOTES ON THE CAPRICES

No. I. For the attainment of exact intonation, it is recommended that this Caprice be studied at first in the following manner:

Very slow practice is essential, and it will be found helpful to repeat each arpeggio at least once, so that the fingers may become well accustomed to the various chord-combinations they must take. They should remain firmly on the strings until they move to the next chord.

Later, and at a somewhat faster tempo, the Caprice should be practised with the following bowings, both of which are excellent studies in bowing technique:

The first of these variants should be taken about half-way between nut and middle, and the second approximately at the middle of the bow. These bowings are intermediate stages of study between the first variant suggested and the continuous sautillé with which the Caprice should eventually be played.

When mastered, this is an effective concert piece. However, it should never be taken at too rapid a tempo; grace, clarity, and variety of tone-color are more effective than a little extra speed.

*See "The Modern Technique of Violin Bowing", by Harold Berkley. G. Schirmer, Inc., New York.

No. II. In the course of study, two bowings should be used in this Caprice: 1) in the upper half of the bow, the detached notes being played martelé, 2) about half-way between nut and middle, the bow leaving the string after each stroke. If the Caprice is practised in this way, great agility of the right arm can be developed. In either bowing, certain passages can be well played only in that part of the bow indicated in the text.

When used in concert, a smoother, semi-detached bowing—in the upper half—should be employed, as a more expressive tone-production can be obtained in this way. A discreet rubato will add greatly to the effectiveness of the performance.

No. V. In the Agitato, Paganini's original bowing is given below the notes. While undoubtedly useful as a bowing exercise, it is of little practical value nowadays owing to its extremely limited possibilities for expression. The Caprice is usually played spiccato, and the modern violinist should be content if he is able to play it cleanly and colorfully with this bowing and at the indicated tempo.

The fingering device given for the descending scales in the opening and closing cadenzas should be carefully noted, for it can be conveniently used in many other compositions.

In order to form a more effective conclusion to the Caprice, the final chromatic scale is often played in the following manner:

No. VI. Probably no finer étude has ever been written for developing strength, independence, and flexibility of the fingers. In the early stages of study, however, it should be practised for only short periods of time, owing to the very exacting demands made on the left hand. At the first sign of tension or fatigue the student should allow his hand to relax completely for fifteen or twenty seconds before resuming his practice. Neglect to do this—or trying, as some players do, to gain so-called endurance by "playing over" a sense of fatigue —may easily result in the development of a chronic muscular stiffness. If, however, the student relaxes his hand at the first feeling of tension, he will soon find that he can remain relaxed for progressively longer periods.

No. IX. Both for study purposes and in concert the scales in the A minor section should be taken as fingered octaves, as follows:

Adding, as they do, both piquancy and color, the harmonics given in the same section should be used when the Caprice is played in public. But when it is in the process of study these notes should be taken, stopped, in the higher positions—for the sake of practice in rapid skips.

The double-harmonic variation of the principal theme should by all means be studied, for two reasons: 1) it is the only passage in these Caprices where double harmonics can conveniently be practised; 2) when well played, the variation adds considerably to the effectiveness of the piece.

No. XIII. Played with or without piano accompaniment, this Caprice is an excellent concert piece. Of the alternative bowings given in the text, the upper is played between the nut and middle of the bow, and the lower between middle and point. Both should be studied, as each has its special qualities musically and technically. In concert performance the upper bowing is perhaps to be preferred, for in expert hands it can give added fire and sparkle to the music.

No. XIV. This excellent chord-study is also effective for concert use. The notes in all the staccato chords should be sounded simultaneously; on the other hand, the legato chords in the third and last two lines may be broken *slightly* in order to permit a sustained, unaccented tone.

No. XVII. When played in concert, the cadenza in the second line is often taken as follows:

Very occasionally, the double-stops in the Da Capo are played in double harmonics. It has not been thought necessary to give this variant here as its use is far-fetched and not to be recommended.

No. XXIV. In performance, the last measure of Variation 4 is usually played in the following manner, in order to connect smoothly with the next Variation:

The bowing given in Variation 8 is much to be preferred to the sustained, alternately Down and Up, bowing very often used. The latter bowing can only be justified if the bridge on the player's violin is so flat that all three strings can be sustained *constantly* throughout the Variation.

On the repetition, the fourth measure of Variation 11 is often elaborated in the following way:

For the sake of an additionally brilliant ending to the Caprice, the final arpeggio can well be extended to four octaves, as follows:

PAGANINI
24 Caprices

Caprices

Study-Version by Harold Berkley

Niccolò Paganini, Op. 1

N = at the nut
M = in the middle
Pt = at the point

L/3 = in the lower third
L/2 = " " " half
U/3 = " " upper third
U/2 = " " " half

I

*See Preface

II

Moderato ♩. = 60

mf dolce

cresc.

dim. *cresc.*

f *mf*

cresc.

f

mf III IV

simile III IV III *cresc.*

f U/2

IV IV

*See Preface

III

V

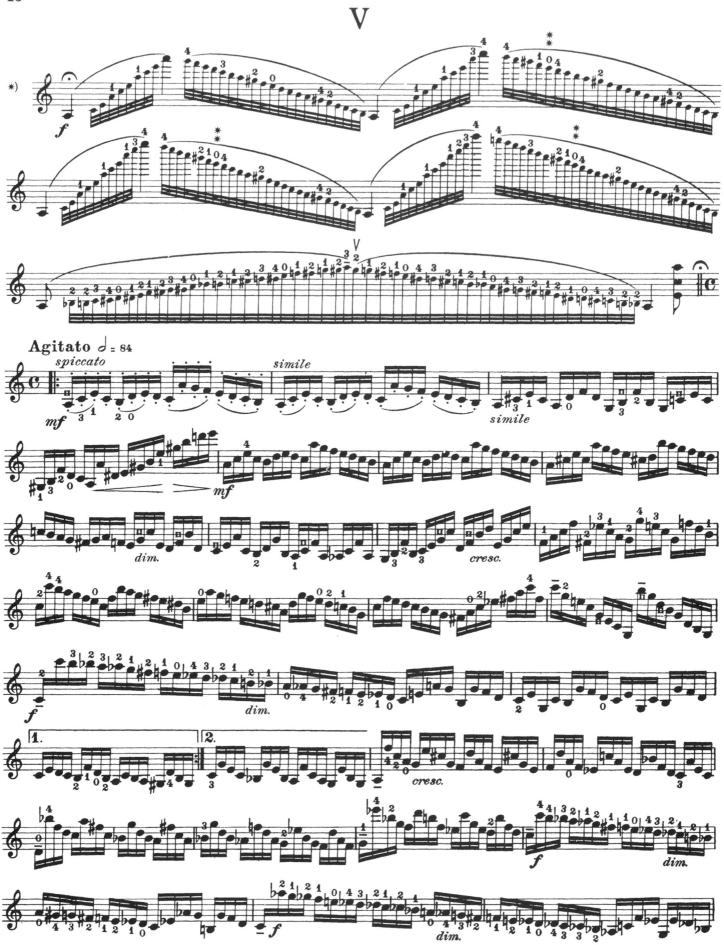

*See Preface

‡ The E indicated by the double asterisks need not be stopped or taken as a harmonic, for at a rapid tempo the open string will sound one octave higher.

** See preceding page.

12

VI

VII

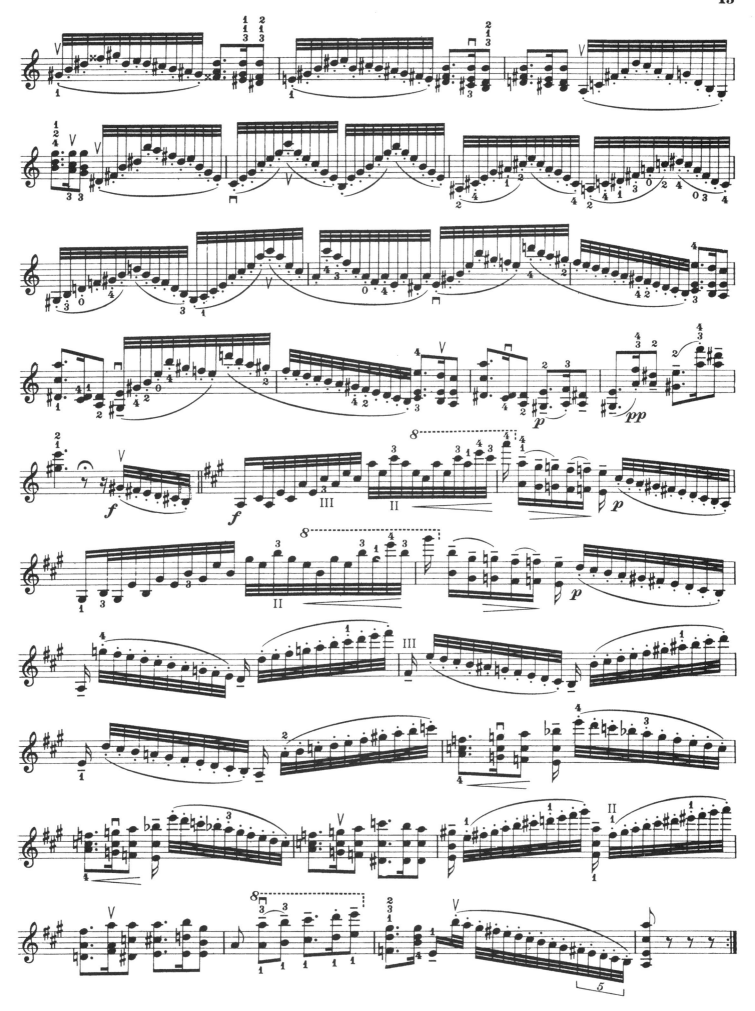

VIII

IX

Allegretto ♩ = 84

X

XI

XII

XIII

Fine

D. C. senza repetizione

*See Preface

XIV

XV

Fine

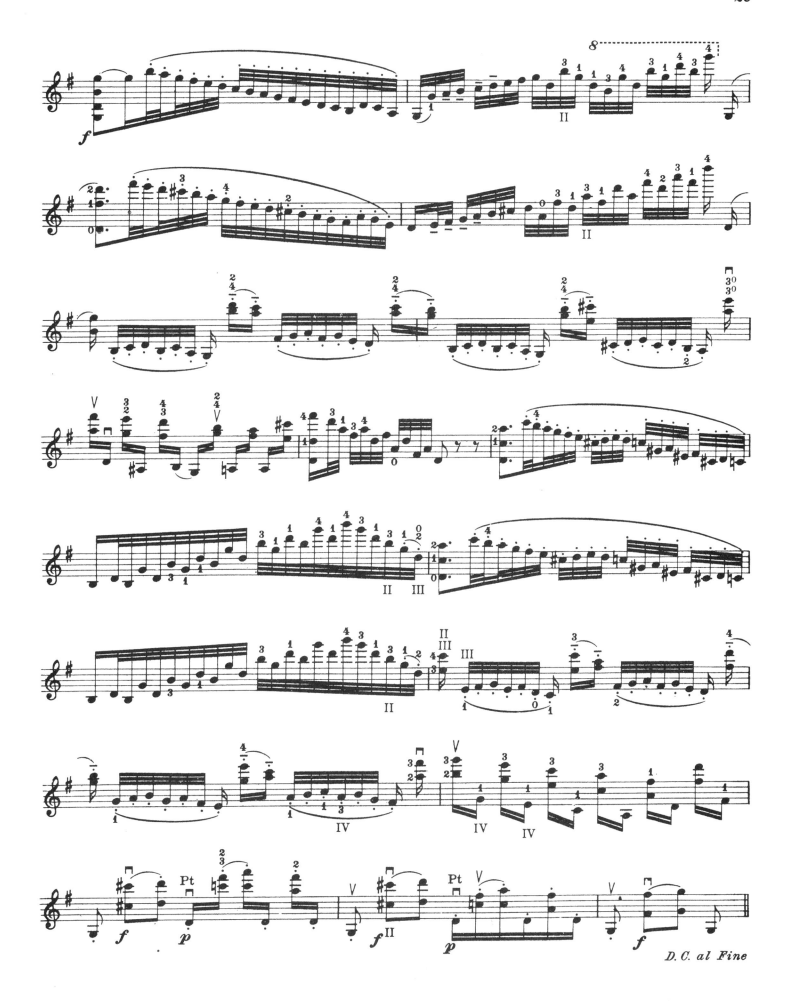

D.C. al Fine

XVI

XVII

Fine

D. C. sin' al Fine senza repetizione

XVIII

D. C. la Corrente

XIX

XX

XXI

Amoroso ♩ = 66

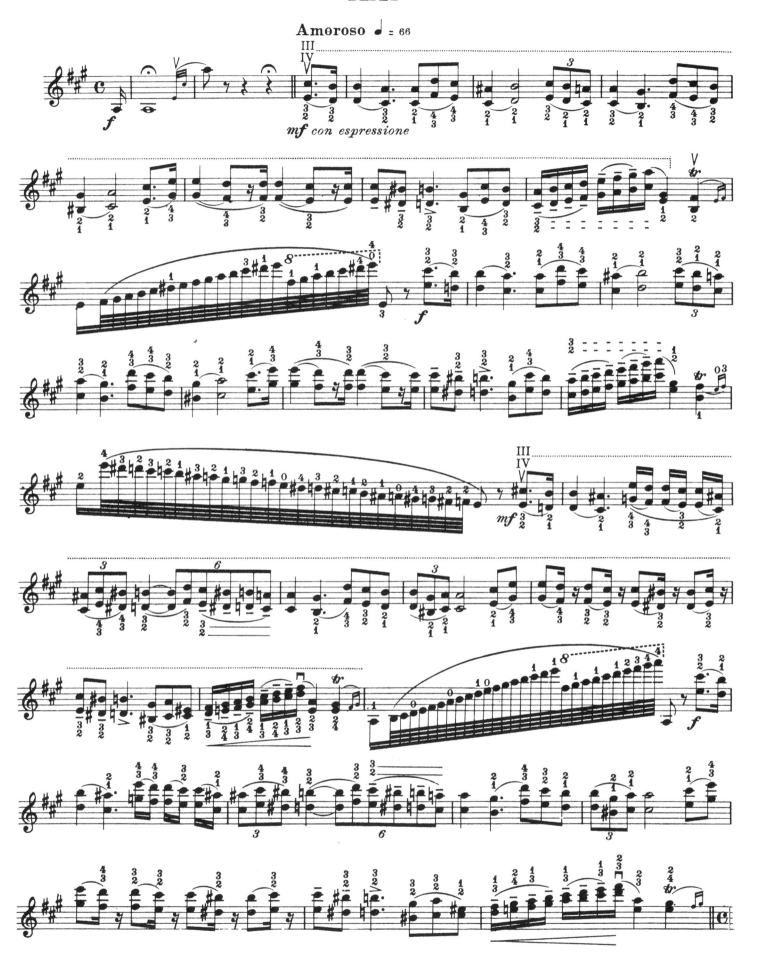

XXII

D.C. al Fine

XXIII